ARTHUR J. LELYVELD
CENTER FOR JEWISH LEARNING

IN MEMORY

OF

JEROME I. POLSTER

By Margie Polster and Children

JEROME I. POLSTER
BOOKSHELF

ANSHE CHESED
FAIRMOUNT TEMPLE

23737 Fairmount Boulevard · Beachwood, Ohio 44122
216.464.1330 · www.fairmounttemple.org

THE BINDING OF
ISAAC

BARBARA COHEN
ILLUSTRATED BY
CHARLES MIKOLAYCAK

LOTHROP, LEE & SHEPARD COMPANY
A Division of William Morrow & Co., Inc.
New York

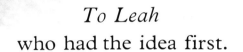

To Leah
who had the idea first.

Text copyright © 1978 by Barbara Cohen
Illustrations copyright © 1978 by Charles Mikolaycak
All rights reserved Printed in the United States of America
First Edition 1 2 3 4 5 6 7 8 9 10
Library of Congress Catalog Number 77-90367
ISBN 0-688-41830-9 ISBN 0-688-51830-3 lib. bdg.

THE GRANDFATHER WAS OLD AND blind. His grandchildren, who sat on his lap and at his feet, listened to him tell what happened when he was a boy.

"When I was two, I no longer nursed at my mother's breast," said the grandfather, whose name was Isaac. "And so my father Abraham made a great feast in honor of my weaning. He invited the chief men of the country to come, and their wives and children, and all their servants. Five hundred people came and they feasted for three days and three nights in my honor. And when they left, they all took with them gifts of wine and olive oil."

"Our father Jacob never made such a feast for me," said Reuben, who was the eldest.

"Oh, well," replied his grandfather, "my father and mother had waited such a long time for me. My father had only two children, Ishmael and me. My father loved Ishmael, but Ishmael hated me."

"Why did he hate you, Grandfather?" asked Judah, who was already as tall and as handsome as a prince.

"Abraham loved our grandfather. Isaac best," explained Joseph, who was dressed in a glorious many-colored coat his father Jacob had given him. "Isn't that so, Grandfather?"

"Just so," said the grandfather, and he nodded. "My father loved me better than Ishmael and for that Ishmael hated me. My mother, Sarah, was my father's true wife, and Ishmael's mother, Hagar, was a servant. Ishmael feared that when our father died, all that he had would come to me. At the weaning feast there were games, and Ishmael shot at targets with his bow and arrow. Sometimes his shot went wild, as if by accident. But Ishmael was a skillful archer. My mother thought his wild shots were not accidents, and she was afraid that one of the arrows would find its way to me. So she asked my father to send Ishmael and his mother away."

"Did he do that?" asked Naphtali, who was also a servant's son. Isaac's grandchildren had the same father, but they had been born of four different mothers. "Did he send his own child away?" Naphtali asked again.

"Yes, he did," said the grandfather. "God told my father He had other plans for Ishmael. My father Abraham sent Ishmael away, although he loved him. For he loved me more. He loved me more than he loved the sun or the moon or the stars."

"He loved you more than he loved anything," said Asher, the plump, generous one.

"No," said the grandfather. "He didn't love me more than anything. But God was afraid he did. God waited, and then one day when I was no longer a baby, God called to my father: 'Abraham.'"

"My father answered, 'Here I am.'

"'Take your son,' God said.

"'But I have two sons,' my father said.

"'Your only son,' God replied.

"'But each is the only one of his mother,' my father said.

"'Whom you love,' God replied.

"'But I love both,' my father said.

"'Even Isaac,' God replied. "Take your son, your only son, whom you love, even Isaac, and go to the land of Moriah, and sacrifice him there to me on the top of the mountain.'"

"But your father wouldn't do that," said Levi. "Not even for God."

"Be quiet and listen," said the grandfather. "Listen to what happened. The next morning my father got up very early. He woke me and told me we were going on a journey. He took two servants with him and a donkey to carry the wood that he had chopped. We traveled through the wilderness for three days. For three days we traveled, and I didn't know where we were going, and I didn't know why."

"Didn't you ask?" Zebulun, who was always curious, wanted to know.

"I asked," the grandfather replied, "and my father told me we were going to make a sacrifice to God. I thought it strange to go so far to make a sacrifice, but my father said God had picked out the place for the sacrifice Himself. I knew that my father talked to God, and that there was no arguing with either of them.

"We came to the bottom of a high mountain, and my father said to his servants, 'Stay here with the donkey. The boy and I will go up to the top of the mountain. There we'll worship God, and then we'll come back to you.'

"My father took the wood we had brought with us from home, and he gave it to me to carry. In one hand he had a pot of coals from our hearth so that he could kindle a fire on the mountain. In the other hand, he carried a knife. We began to climb the mountain, both of us together."

"It seemed strange to me—wood, fire, knife, but no calf or lamb or kid to offer to God. So I said, 'My father.'

"And he answered me, 'Here I am, my son.'

"And I said, 'Here's the fire, and here's the wood, but where's the lamb to offer to God?'

"My father answered me, 'God will provide the lamb for the offering, my son.'

"So we climbed and climbed, both of us together. When we got to the top of the mountain, my father placed some large stones on top of piles of smaller stones to make an altar. He took the wood that I had carried and laid a fire in the altar. Still there was no sign of a calf or a lamb or a kid, and I said to my father once again, 'Where's the lamb to offer to God?'

"Then my father said, 'You are the lamb, my son.' And he laid me down on the altar, and he took rope and tied me there so that I couldn't move."

"Didn't you cry? Didn't you scream? Didn't you struggle?" urged Gad, who was a fighter.

"There was such sadness in my father's eyes," the grandfather went on in a dreamy voice as if he hadn't even heard the question. "He moved so slowly, so heavily. I didn't make a sound. I didn't make a move. I couldn't."

The grandfather paused for a moment, and his strong old arm tightened around Benjamin, who was the baby and sat on his lap.

For a little while, none of the children spoke. Then Simeon said, "My father would never do that to me. Even if God did ask him to."

"Well, God didn't ask your father to," the

grandfather replied sharply. "He's asked it of no one else since."

"Don't be angry with me, Grandfather," said Simeon.

"I'm not angry, Simeon," said the grandfather in a gentler voice. "I know how you feel. I couldn't believe my father would do it to me either. And if he could, then what was the use of living? And that's why I lay there so quiet and so still. I didn't believe it was happening. Even when my father took the knife in his hand, and stretched forth his arm, and the tip of the knife touched my chest, I didn't believe it."

"What happened then, Grandfather?" asked Dan, the logical one. "You're here today to tell us the story, so you didn't die."

"Something died," the grandfather replied. "I didn't die; only something in me died. Then a voice called out from heaven. 'Abraham, Abraham,' the voice called. It was God's voice.

"'Here I am,' my father replied.

"'Don't touch the boy,' the voice said. 'Don't touch him with the knife or with your hand. I know now you love Me more than anything, because you were willing to give Me your son, your only son.'

"Then my father stood up. In the bushes he saw a ram, caught by the horns. My father untied me, and we took the ram and bound it to the altar. With his knife, my father killed the ram, and then we lit the fire and made an offering of the ram to God.

"The voice of God spoke to my father again. This time God said, 'Because you have done this thing, because you have been willing to give Me your son, your only son, you will be blessed. You will have as many great-great-great-great grandchildren as there are stars in the sky and grains of sand upon the shore. Because you listened to Me, your great-great-great-great grandchildren shall rule whole cities and bring blessings to all the people of the earth.'"

"And will all that happen?" asked Judah, the prince.

"Yes," replied their grandfather Isaac. "All that will happen—if not to you, then to those who come after you. And none of you will ever be asked to sacrifice your children. God will not ask anyone to do that again. That's the promise he made to my father, Abraham, and to me."

"But Grandfather," said Dinah, who was the only girl, "if the voice of God had not come out of heaven and told your father not to sacrifice you, do you think he would have? Do you think your father would have killed you?"

"I don't know," replied the grandfather. "And since I didn't know, that question stood between me and my father as long as he lived. On the way home, he told me how God had commanded him to sacrifice me, but I never asked him if he really would have done it, and he never told me."

"We do what we must do," said Issachar, who worked hard in the fields. "Our great-grandfather Abraham had sworn to serve God in every way. He had to do what God told him to do."

"I don't think he would have done it,"

19-149

Dinah insisted. "What would he have said to Sarah when he came back if our grandfather Isaac had not been with him? And God didn't think he'd do it either. And God didn't want to find out, for sure."

The grandfather smiled. "God must have known, Dinah. But I never knew, and even my father couldn't be sure. But God—God knows. And my father and I—we had to be content with not knowing. My father and I, and all of you—in the end what we do is what God wills us to do."

"The important thing, Grandfather," said Joseph, the dreamer who dreamed the truth, "is that you didn't die. You didn't die. You lived. You are here."

"That's right, Joseph," his grandfather said to him. "That's the important thing."

BARBARA COHEN, perhaps best known for that little classic *The Carp in the Bathtub,* is also highly regarded for her novels, which include *Thank You, Jackie Robinson, Benny,* and *Bitter Herbs and Honey.* Mrs. Cohen, a newspaper columnist and former English teacher as well as novelist, grew up in New Jersey in an inn operated by her widowed mother. Today, with her husband Gene and their three daughters, she still lives in the same vicinity.

CHARLES MIKOLAYCAK, a distinguished graphics designer and illustrator, has received many honors for his children's books, some of which have been ALA Notables and Children's Book Council Showcase selections. He and his wife Carole, a magazine picture editor, live in New York City.

FREUD AND THE NON-EUROPEAN

FREUD AND THE NON-EUROPEAN

$\blacklozenge$

EDWARD W. SAID

With an introduction by CHRISTOPHER BOLLAS
and a response by JACQUELINE ROSE

Published in association with the Freud Museum, London

VERSO
London · New York

First published by Verso, in association with the
Freud Museum, London, 2003
FREUD AND THE NON-EUROPEAN
Copyright © 2003 Edward W. Said
Introductions © 2003 by Christopher Bollas
Response © 2003 by Jacqueline Rose

1 3 5 7 9 10 8 6 4 2

Verso
UK: 6 Meard Street, London W1F 0EG
USA: 180 Varick Street, New York, NY 10014–4606
www.versobooks.com

Verso is the imprint of New Left Books

ISBN 1–85984–500–2

British Library Cataloguing in Publication Data
A catalogue record for this book is available from the British Library

Library of Congress Cataloging-in-Publication Data
A catalog record for this book is available from the Library of Congress

Typeset in Garamond by YHT
Printed and bound in the USA by R.R. Donnelley & Sons

CONTENTS

INTRODUCING EDWARD SAID

Christopher Bollas

On behalf of the Freud Museum of London I am pleased to welcome all of you to this important occasion: to hear Professor Edward Said's talk on "Freud and the Non-European", to be discussed later by Professor Jacqueline Rose, whom I shall introduce before her response.

Well, it is no new experience for Edward Said to be in exile, and so it is here, following in Freud's footsteps (in certain respects), that he is to speak in London rather than Vienna; but those who have studied with him, or know him personally, well appreciate his remarkable yet natural way of transforming injustice into learned protest. "Provided that the exile refuses to sit on the sidelines nursing a wound," he writes in *Reflections on Exile*, "there are things to be learned: he or she must cultivate a scrupulous (not indulgent or sulky) subjectivity."[1]

Said was born in West Jerusalem of parents who

ordinarily resided in Cairo but travelled to Palestine often to see family and friends. His first deep contact with the fate of the exile was in 1948, when his family was driven from Palestine, and he was not to return for forty-five years. Perhaps it was his Aunt Nabiha's energy and determination to address the "desolations of being without a country or a place to return to" that inscribed itself in that gathering momentum that was to become Said the international figure, but he has alluded to the importance of his move to the United States – first to boarding school, and then to Princeton University – which not only widened his horizons, but became an "object to be used", if I may allude to Winnicott's notion of creativity and the use of the object through which further to articulate his remarkable sensibility.

At Columbia University as a young assistant professor, he wrote his first book on Joseph Conrad (1966),[2] and between then and now I think he has written at least twenty books, translated into over thirty-six languages.

The 1967 war shook him from even an imaginary future in the academic ivory tower, and this event sponsored a new line of thought in his life that would realize itself most clearly in his book *Orientalism*, which examined, among other things, European writings on the Orient, illuminating the politics of literary representation. But *Beginnings* (1975) was certainly his first — I hate to say this — intellectual "collateral response" to that war. Said now had to begin again — not consciously knowing, perhaps, where he was headed, but knowing that his life, though influenced by forces beyond him, was evoking his own fierce response. "My view is that an intensified, even irritated, awareness of what really goes on when we begin, that is, when we are conscious of beginning, actually projects the task in a very particular way."[3]

(Those of you here who are interested in psychoanalytical studies will want to read his analysis of Freud's *Interpretation of Dreams* in *Beginnings*, as I think it is a fascinating literary analysis of Freud's book as enacting what it argues.)

In 1977 Said was elected to the Palestine National Council, where he remained until 1991, when he resigned. As most of you here know, he has been a brilliant, tireless and courageous spokesman for the Palestinian cause. *The Question of Palestine* was published in 1979.[4] Its topics include the psychology of the refusal to recognize an other's being, or to think psychoanalytically about the question he raises; it invites us to consider the effects of "negative hallucination": of not seeing the existence of an object or an other. Thus in examining the structure of oppression, we must not only look at what the oppressors project into the oppressed (for example, Israeli violence projected into the Palestinian people), but we must also take into account a refusal to recognize the actual existence of this other (in this case Israel's reluctance to recognize the existence of Palestinians). It is this combination of positive and negative hallucination which makes this object relation, as we would call it in psychoanalysis, not only toxic but psychotic. The oppressed exists, in this respect, to contain unwanted destructiveness in the oppressor who insists at the same time that the oppressed be like a fecal entity that is so odious that it cannot be recognized, except if and when it is out of sight, and finally eliminated. In many respects, Said's writings not only constitute a literary resistence to the "intellectual genocide"[5] that takes place in too many Western narratives about the Palestinian, but simultaneously function as a resistance to a schizophrenogenic imposition. The stone-throwing Palestinian is symbolically returning that Israeli violence that has used stones to build the settlements. The horror of the suicide bomber returns the violence of Israeli guns, tanks and warplanes. The aim of such resistance is not to overcome Israel, it is to return Israel to itself, for better and for worse. Palesti-

nian violence seeks to maintain sanity for its people through the insistence that the self exists even as the oppressors seek to deny it, something that, of course, the Jewish people know only too well through the catastrophe that was the Holocaust.

Some of his subsequent writings examine the provincialism of academic studies, or what we might think of as the provincialist defence against the multicultural: in psychoanalysis, a form of splitting of the ego in which any self resides happily inside a mere fragment of itself, in order to remain untroubled by all the other parts of the total picture.

Edward Said is also a fine pianist, and became the music critic of a prominent American publication, *The Nation*. He has collaborated with Daniel Barenboim and the Chicago Symphony Orchestra in a new production of Beethoven's *Fidelio*, for which he wrote a new English text to replace the spoken dialogue; in addition, he conducted a workshop with Barenboim and Yo-Yo Ma for young Arab and Israeli musicians in Weimar, Germany. He has written on many musical subjects, his essays on Glenn Gould are wonderful, and he has taken a musical act – the "contrapuntal" – and put it into the world of political and literary discourse:

Most people are principally aware of one culture, one setting, one home; exiles are aware of at least two, and this plurality of vision gives rise to an awareness of simultaneous dimensions, an awareness that, to borrow a phrase from music, is *contrapuntal*. For an exile, habits of life, expression, or activity in the new environment inevitably occur against the memory of these things in another environment.[6]

We could certainly "transfer" *his invention* to psychoanalytical theory, proposing the "psychic contrapuntal" which recognizes the benefit of movement outside of one's primary place, to a new location from which the self, and its others, are seen in a different light. Moving from the maternal order to the paternal order, from the image-sense world of the infantile place to the symbolic order of language, may be our first taste of exile, one that seems to haunt and yet energize much of Proust's writing. In this respect, we may all be exiles of a sort — perhaps this is why even those of us who have not shared the terrible fate of those driven from home can none the less grasp their fate empathically.

Edward Said is a University Professor at Columbia University. He has delivered the Reith Lectures for the

BBC, the Rene Wellek Memorial Lectures at the University of California-Irvine, the Henry Stafford Little Lecture at Princeton, and the Empson Lectures at Cambridge University. He is a member of the American Academy of Arts and Sciences, the Royal Society of Literature, The American Philosophical Society, and the American Academy of Arts and Letters. He has received honorary doctorates from sixteen universities. He is the recipient of too many prizes and awards to name here, but I must mention that his memoir *Out of Place* won the 1999 *New Yorker* Book Award for Non-Fiction. He also won the 2000 Ainsfield–Wolf Book Award for Non-Fiction, the Morton Dauwen Zabel Award in Literature conferred by the American Academy of Arts and Letters, and the 2001 Lannan Literary Award for Lifetime Achievement. His most recent publications include *The End of the Peace Process: Oslo and After*; *Reflections on Exile and Other Essays*; and *Power, Politics and Culture*.[7] He is currently working on *The Relevance of Humanism in Contemporary America*, to be published in 2002 by Columbia University Press.

FREUD AND THE NON-EUROPEAN

Edward W. Said

There are two ways in which I shall be using the term "non-European" in this lecture – one that applies to Freud's own time; the other to the period after his death in 1939. Both are deeply relevant to a reading of his work today. One, of course, is a simple designation of the world beyond Freud's own as a Viennese-Jewish scientist, philosopher and intellectual who lived and worked his entire life in either Austria or England. No one who has read and been influenced by Freud's extraordinary work has failed to be impressed by the remarkable range of his erudition, especially in literature and the history of culture. But by the same token, one is very struck by the fact that beyond the confines of Europe, Freud's awareness of other cultures (with perhaps one exception, that of Egypt) is inflected, and, indeed shaped by his education in the Judaeo-Christian tradition, particularly the humanistic and scientific assumptions that give it its peculiarly "Western" stamp. This is something that doesn't so much limit Freud in an uninteresting way as identify him as belonging to a place and time that were still not tremendously bothered by what today, in the current postmodern, post-structuralist, postcolonialist jargon, we would call the problems of the Other. Of course Freud was deeply gripped by what stands outside the limits of reason, convention, and, of course, consciousness: his whole work in that sense is about the Other, but always about an Other recognizable mainly to readers who are well acquainted with the classics of Graeco-Roman and Hebrew Antiquity and what was later to derive from them in the various modern European languages, literatures, sciences, religions and cultures with which he himself was well acquainted.

Like most of his contemporaries, Freud knew that other, noteworthy cultures existed and deserved recognition. He referred to those of India and China, for instance, but only in passing and only when, say, the practice of dream interpretation there might be of comparative interest to the European investigator of the subject. Much more frequent are Freud's references to the "primitive" non-European cultures — mostly via James Frazer — on which he drew for his discussion of early religious practices. These references provide most of the substance for *Totem and Taboo*,[8] but Freud's ethnographic curiosity hardly goes beyond looking at and citing aspects of these cultures (sometimes with a numbing repetitiveness) as supporting evidence for his argument about such matters as defilement, prohibitions against incest, and patterns of exogamy and endogamy. To Freud, the Pacific, Australian and African cultures he took so much from had been pretty much left behind or forgotten, like the primal horde, in the march of civilization; and even though we know how much of Freud's work is dedicated to recovering and acknowledging what has either been forgotten or won't be admitted, I don't think that in cultural terms non-European primitive peoples and cultures were as fascinating to him as were the people and stories of Ancient Greece, Rome and Israel. The latter were his real predecessors in terms of psychoanalytic images and concepts.

Nevertheless, in view of the dominant race theories of the time, Freud had his own ideas about non-European outsiders, most notably Moses and Hannibal. Both were Semites, of course, and both (especially Hannibal) were heroes for Freud because of their audacity, persistence and courage. Reading *Moses and Monotheism*,[9] one is struck by Freud's almost casual assumption (which also applies to Hannibal) that Semites were most certainly not European (in fact, Hannibal spends his life fruitlessly trying to conquer Rome, but never even gets there) and, at the same time, were somehow assimilable to its culture as former outsiders. This is quite different from theories about Semites propounded by Orientalists like Renan and racial thinkers such as Gobineau and Wagner, who underlined the foreignness and excludability of Jews – as well as Arabs, for that matter – to Graeco-Germanic-Aryan culture. Freud's view of Moses as both insider and outsider is extraordinarily interesting and challenging, I think, but I want to talk about this later. In any event, I believe it is true to say that Freud's was a Eurocentric view of culture – and why should it not be? His world had not yet been touched by the globalization, or rapid travel, or decolonization, that were to make many formerly unknown or repressed cultures available to metropolitan Europe. He lived just before the massive population shifts that were to bring Indians, Africans, West Indians, Turks and Kurds into the heart of Europe as guest-workers and often unwelcome immigrants. And, of course, he died just as the Austro-Germanic and Roman world portrayed so memorably by great contemporaries such as Thomas Mann and Romain Rolland would lie in ruins, with millions of his fellow Jews slaughtered by the Nazi Reich. In effect, it was also the world commemorated in Erich Auerbach's *Mimesis*, the autumnal exilic book written during the war years in Istanbul, whence this great *Gelehrter* and philologist could sum up the passing of a tradition seen in its coherent wholeness for the last time.

The second – and far more politically charged – meaning of "the non-European" that I'd like to draw attention to is the culture that emerged historically in the post-World-War-Two period – that is, after the fall of the classical empires and the emergence of many newly liberated peoples and states in Africa, Asia and the Americas. Obviously, I cannot go into the many new configurations of power, people and politics that have resulted, but I would like to stress one in particular that seems to me to give a rather fascinating perspective, and indeed enhances the radicality of Freud's work on human identity. What I have in mind is how, in the postwar world, that constellation of words and valences that surrounds Europe and the West acquired a much more fraught and even rebarbative meaning from observers outside Europe and the West. Because of the Cold War there were first of all two Europes, East and West; and then, in the peripheral regions of the world going through the throes of decolonization, there was the Europe that was representative of the great empires, now seething with insurrections that were finally to develop into struggles beyond European and Western control. Elsewhere I have tried to describe the new light in which Europe is now seen by articulate anticolonial combatants, so I won't go into it here, except briefly to quote Fanon – surely Freud's most disputatious heir – from the final pages of his last, posthumously published book, *The Wretched of the Earth*.[10] The section I shall be citing is one of the appendices to the book entitled "Colonial Wars and Mental Disorders", in which – as you will recall – Fanon catalogues and comments on a series of cases he has dealt with that emanate, as it were, from the colonial battlefield.

First of all, he notes that to the European, the non-European world contains only natives, and "the veiled women, the palm trees and the camels make up the landscape, the *natural* background to the human presence of the French".[11] After listing how the native is diagnosed by the European clinical psychiatrist as a savage killer who kills for no reason, Fanon cites a Professor A. Porot, whose considered scientific opinion is that the native's life is dominated by "diencephalic urges" whose net result is an undevelopable primitivism.

Here Fanon quotes a chilling passage from a learned technical psychiatric analysis by Professor Porot himself:

This primitivism is not merely a way of living which is the result of a special upbringing; it has much deeper roots. We even consider that it must have its substratum in a particular predisposition of the architectonic structure, or at least in the dynamic hierarchization of the nervous centers. We are in the presence of a coherent body of comportment and of a coherent life which can be explained scientifically. The Algerian has no cortex; or, more precisely, he is dominated, like the inferior vertebrates, by the diencephalons. The cortical functions, if they exist at all, are very feeble, and are practically unintegrated into the dynamic of existence.[12]

While it may be possible to see in this sort of thing a fundamentalist perversion of Freud's description of primitive behaviour in *Totem and Taboo*, what seems to be missing is Freud's implicit refusal, in the end, to erect an insurmountable barrier between non-European primitives and European civilization; on the contrary, the severity of Freud's argument, as I read it, is that what may have been left behind historically catches up with us in such universal behaviours as the prohibition against incest, or – as he characterizes it in *Moses and Monotheism* – the return of the repressed. Of course, Freud posits a qualitative difference between primitive and civilized that seems to work to the latter's advantage, but that difference, as in the fiction of his equally gifted subversive contemporary Joseph Conrad, doesn't excuse or in any way mitigate the rigour of his analyses of civilization itself, which he sees in a decidedly ambiguous, even pessimistic, way.

The point for Fanon, though, is that when you extend not just Freud, but all the scientific achievements of European science, into the practice of colonialism, Europe ceases to occupy a normative position with regard to the native. Hence, Fanon proclaims:

leave this Europe where they are never done talking of Man, yet murder men everywhere they find them, at the corner of every one of their own streets, in all the corners of the globe. . . . Europe undertook the leadership of the world with ardor, cynicism, and violence. Look at how the shadow of her palaces stretches out ever further! Every one of her movements has burst the bounds of space and thought.

Europe has declined all humility and all modesty; but she has also set her face against all solicitude and tenderness. ... When I search for Man in the technique and the style of Europe, I see only a succession of negations of man, and an avalanche of murders.

Not surprisingly, then, and even though his prose and some of his reasoning depend on it, Fanon rejects the European model entirely, and demands instead that all human beings collaborate together in the invention of new ways to create what he calls "the new man, whom Europe has been incapable of bringing to triumphant birth".[13]

Fanon himself scarcely provides his readers with anything like a blueprint for the new ways he has in mind; his main purpose, however, is to indict Europe for having divided human beings into a hierarchy of races that reduced and dehumanized the subordinates to both the scientific gaze and the will of the superiors. The actualization of the scheme, of course, is what was brought forth by the colonial system in the imperial domains, but I think it is true to say that the gist of Fanon's attack was to include the whole edifice of European humanism itself, which proved incapable of going beyond its own invidious limitations of vision. As Immanuel Wallerstein described so well,[14] subsequent critics of Eurocentrism in the last four decades of the twentieth century furthered the attack by taking on Europe's historiography, the claims of its universalism, its definition of civilization, its Orientalism, and its uncritical acceptance of a paradigm of progress that placed what Huntington and others like him have called "the West" at the centre of an encroaching mass of lesser civilizations trying to challenge the West's supremacy.

However much or little one agrees with Fanon or Wallerstein, there is no doubt that the whole idea of cultural difference itself – especially today – is far from the inert thing taken for granted by Freud. The notion that there were other cultures besides that of Europe about which one needed to think is really not the animating principle for his work that it was in Fanon's, any more than it was for the major work of his contemporaries Thomas Mann, Romain Rolland and Erich Auerbach. Of the four, Auerbach was the one who survived somewhat into the postcolonial era, but he was mystified – perhaps even a little depressed – by what he could intimate of what was coming. In his late essay "Philologie der Weltliteratur" he spoke elegiacally of the replacement of Romania as the research paradigm that had nourished his own career by a welter of what he called "new" languages and cultures, without realizing that many of them in Asia and Africa were older than those of Europe, and had well-established canons and philologies that European scholars of his generation simply never knew existed. At any rate, Auerbach had the capacity to sense that a new historical era was being born, and he could tell that its lineaments and structures would be unfamiliar precisely because so much in it was neither European nor Eurocentric.

I feel I should add something else here. I have often been interpreted as retrospectively attacking great writers and thinkers like Jane Austen and Karl Marx because some of their ideas seem politically incorrect by the standards of our time. That is a stupid notion which, I just have to say categorically, is not true of anything I have either written or said. On the contrary, I am always trying to understand figures from the past whom I admire, even as I point out how bound they were by the perspectives of their own cultural moment as far as their views of other cultures and peoples were concerned. The special point I then try to make is that it is imperative to read them as intrinsically worthwhile for today's non-European or non-Western reader, who is often either happy to dismiss them altogether as dehumanizing or

Conrad portrays in terms that Achebe finds so objectionable not only contain within them the frozen essence that condemns them to the servitude and punishment Conrad sees as their present fate, but also point prophetically towards a whole series of implied developments that their later history discloses despite, over and above, and also paradoxically because of, the radical severity and awful solitude of Conrad's essentializing vision. The fact that later writers keep returning to Conrad means that his work, by virtue of its uncompromising Eurocentric vision, is precisely what gives it its antinomian force, the intensity and power wrapped inside its sentences, which demand an equal and opposite response to meet them head on in a confirmation, a refutation, or an elaboration of what they present. In the grip of Conrad's Africa, you are driven by its sheer stifling horror to work through it, to push beyond it as history itself transforms even the most unyielding stasis into process and a search for greater clarity, relief, resolution or denial. And of course in Conrad, as with all such extraordinary minds, the felt tension between what is intolerably there and a symmetrical compulsion to escape from it is what is most profoundly at stake – what the reading and interpretation of a work like *Heart of Darkness* is all about. Texts that are inertly of their time stay there: those which brush up unstintingly against historical constraints are the ones we keep with us, generation after generation.

Freud is a remarkable instance of a thinker for whom scientific work was, as he often said, a kind of archaeological excavation of the buried, forgotten, repressed and denied past. Not for nothing was Schliemann a model for him.[15] Freud was an explorer of the mind, of course, but also, in the philosophical sense, an overturner and a re-mapper of accepted or settled geographies and genealogies. He thus lends himself especially to rereading in different contexts, since his work is all about how life history offers itself by recollection, research and reflection to endless structuring and restructuring, in both the individual and the collective sense. That we, different readers from different periods of history, with different cultural backgrounds, should continue to do this in our readings of Freud strikes me as nothing less than a vindication of his work's power to instigate new thought, as well as to illuminate situations that he himself might never have dreamed of.

Freud's intense concentration on Moses occupied the last months of his life, and what he produced in his last major book, *Moses and Monotheism*, is a composite of several texts, numerous intentions, different periods of time – all of them personally difficult for him in view of his illness, the advent of National Socialism and the political uncertainties of his life in Vienna which meant that he had to contend with sometimes contradictory and even disorganizing, destabilizing effects.[16] Anyone with an interest in what has been called late style [*Spätstil*] will find in Freud's *Moses* an almost classic example. Like the bristlingly difficult works that Beethoven produced in the last seven or eight years of his life – the last five piano sonatas, the final quartets, the *Missa Solemnis*, the Choral Symphony, and the Opus 119 and 121 Bagatelles – *Moses* seems to be composed by Freud for himself, with scant attention to frequent and often ungainly repetition, or regard for elegant economy of prose and exposition. In this book, Freud the scientist looking for objective results in his investigation, and Freud the Jewish intellectual probing his own relationship with his ancient faith through the history and identity of its founder, are never really brought into a tidy fit with each other. Everything about the treatise suggests not resolution and reconciliation – as in some late works such as *The Tempest* or *The Winter's Tale* – but, rather, more complexity and a willingness to let irreconcilable elements of the work remain as they are: episodic, fragmentary, unfinished (i.e. unpolished).

In Beethoven's case and in Freud's, as I hope to show, the intellectual trajectory conveyed by the late work is intransigence and a sort of irascible transgressiveness, as if the author was expected to settle down into a harmonious composure, as befits a person at the end of his life, but preferred instead to be difficult, and to bristle with all sorts of new ideas and provocations. Freud explicitly confesses to this unseemliness in a footnote early in *Moses* where, without embarrassment, he refers to his autocratic, arbitrary and even unscrupulous way with biblical evidence. There are also explicit reminders to the reader that the author is an old man, and may not be up to his task; at the end of the second part and the beginning of the third Freud draws attention to his failing strength as well as to the diminishment in his creative powers. But this admission doesn't stop or in any way deter him from reaching difficult and often mystifyingly unsatisfactory conclusions. Like Beethoven's late works, Freud's *Spätwerk* is obsessed with returning not just to the problem of Moses's identity – which, of course, is at the very core of the treatise – but to the very elements of identity itself, as if that issue so crucial to psychoanalysis, the very heart of the science, could be returned to in the way that Beethoven's late work returns to such basics as tonality and rhythm.

Moreover, the combination in Freud of interest in the contemporary expressed in sometimes arcane excavations of the primordial are parallel to Beethoven's use of medieval modes and startlingly advanced counterpoint in works like the *Missa Solemnis*. Above all, late style's effect on the reader or listener is alienating – that is to say, Freud and Beethoven present material that is of pressing concern to them with scant regard for satisfying, much less placating, the reader's need for closure. Other books by Freud were written with a didactic or pedagogic aim in mind: *Moses and Monotheism* is not. Reading the treatise, we feel that Freud wishes us to understand that there are other issues at stake here – other, more pressing problems to expose than ones whose solution might be comforting, or provide a sort of resting-place.

In one of the most interesting of several books on Freud's *Moses* – Josef Yerushalmi's *Freud's Moses: Judaism Terminable and Interminable*[17] – Yerushalmi expertly fills in the personal Jewish background to Freud's probing of the Moses story, including his painfully longstanding awareness of anti-Semitism in such episodes as his spoiled friendship with Carl Jung, his disappointment with his father's inability to stand up to insults, his concern that psychoanalysis might be considered only a

"Jewish" science, and, centrally, his own complicated and, in my opinion, hopelessly unresolved connection to his own Jewishness, which he seemed always to hold on to with a combination of pride and defiance. Yet Freud repeats over and over that although he was a Jew he did not believe in God, and only in the most minimal way could be said to have any religious sense at all. Yerushalmi shrewdly points out that Freud seemed to have believed, perhaps following Lamarck, that "the character traits embedded in the Jewish psyche are themselves transmitted phylogenetically and no longer require religion in order to be sustained. On such a final Lamarckian assumption even godless Jews like Freud inevitably inherit and share them". So far so good. But then Yerushalmi goes on to ascribe a kind of almost desperately providential leap to Freud that I find largely unwarranted. "If monotheism", he says, "was genetically Egyptian, it has been historically Jewish". He then adds – quoting Freud – that "it is honor enough for the Jewish people that it kept alive such a tradition and produced men who lent it their voice, *even if the stimulus had first come from the outside, from a great stranger*" (italics added).[18]

This is so central a point in Freud's argument that it bears looking into further; certainly, I think, Yerushalmi has jumped to conclusions about what is historically Jewish that Freud himself doesn't actually reach because, as I shall try to show, the actual Jewishness that derives from Moses is a far from open-and-shut matter, and is in fact extremely problematic. Freud is resolutely divided about it; indeed, I would go so far as to say that he is deliberately antinomian in his beliefs. You will recall that Freud's opening sentence is an astonishingly hybristic celebration of what he has done and will do in the pages that follow, which is nothing less than "to deny a people the man whom it praises as the greatest of its sons"; he then goes on to say that a feat of this kind cannot be entered into gladly or carelessly, "especially by one belonging to that people". He does so in the interests of a truth – he minces no words at all – far more important than what are "supposed [to be] national interests". The sarcasm in this last phrase fairly takes your breath away, as much for its arrogance as for its willingness to subordinate the interests of a whole people to what is more important: the removal of a religion's source from its place inside the community and history of like-minded believers.[19]

I won't rehearse all the main points of Freud's arguments – I too wish to be a bit arbitrary – except to recall emphases that he makes in them. First, of course, is

Moses's Egyptian identity, and the fact that his ideas about a single God are derived entirely from the Egyptian Pharaoh, who is universally credited with the invention of monotheism. Unlike Yerushalmi, for instance, Freud goes out of his way to credit Akhenaton with this idea, insisting that it was an invention which did not exist before him; and although he says that monotheism did not take root in Egypt, Freud must have known perfectly well that monotheism returned to Egypt first in the form of primitive Christianity (which remains in the Coptic Church of today) and then via Islam, which he does in fact discuss briefly later in the text. Recent work in Egyptology in fact suggests that considerable traces of monotheism are found well before Akhenaton's reign, and this in turn suggests that Egypt's role in the development of the worship of one God is a good deal more significant than has often been allowed. Yerushalmi is far more anxious than Freud to scrape away all traces of monotheism from Egypt after Akhenaton's death, and he implies that it was the genius of Judaism to have elaborated the religion well beyond anything the Egyptians knew about.

Freud, however, is more complex, and even contradictory. He grants that the Jews eliminated sun-worship from the religion they took over from Akhenaton, but further undercuts Judaic originality by noting (a) that circumcision was an Egyptian, not a Hebrew, idea; and (b) that the Levites, surely as Judaic a group as convention says ever existed, were Moses's Egyptian followers, who had come along with him to the new place.

As for that place, Freud departs further from the conventionally attributed Israelite geography and states that it was Meribat-Qades: "in the country south of Palestine between the eastern end of the Sinai peninsula and the western end of Arabia. There they took over the worship of a god Jahve, probably from the neighbouring Arabian tribe of Midianites. Presumably other neighbouring tribes were also followers of that God".[20] So Freud first restores to their place components of the origin of Judaism that had been forgotten or denied along with the murder of the heroic father common to all religions, then shows − via his theory of dormancy and the return of the repressed − how Judaism constituted itself as a permanently established religion. The argument is strangely subtle and discontinuous, as anyone who has read *Moses and Monotheism* will quickly attest. Repression, denial and return pass before the reader almost magically as experiences from the individual to the collective: they are arrayed by Freud in a sequence of narrative followed by submerged and then manifest positivity, all of which gives rise not only to Jewishness but to the anti-Semitism that goes along with it. The main points I want to underscore are first, that all of this is given an entirely secular setting by Freud, with no concession made that I have been able to find to the divine or the extra-historical; and second, that Freud makes no effort to smooth out his story or give it a clear trajectory. This is perhaps because so much of the material he is dealing with as he chronicles the aftermath of Moses's legacy is uneven, as radically antithetical in its startlingly sharp contrast between the founding outsider and the community he established (which also killed him) as the primal words he had studied and written about decades earlier.

On one level, this is no more than to say that the elements of historical identity seem always to be composite, particularly when seminal events like the killing of the father and the exodus from Egypt are themselves so tied up in prior events. As to whether Moses can be said to be "foreign" to the Jews who adopt him as their patriarch, Freud is quite clear, even adamant: Moses was an Egyptian, and was therefore different from the people who adopted him as their leader – people, that is, who became the Jews whom Moses seems to have later created as *his* people. To say of Freud's relationship with

Judaism that it was conflicted is to venture an under-statement. At times he was proud of his belonging, even though he was irremediably anti-religious; at other times he expressed annoyance with and unmistakable disapproval of Zionism. In a famous letter about the work of the Jewish Agency in 1930, for instance, he refused to join in an appeal to the British to increase Jewish immigration to Palestine. In fact he went so far as to condemn the transformation "of a piece of Herodian wall into a national relic, thus offending the feelings of the natives". Five years later, having accepted a position on the board of the Hebrew University, he told the Jewish National Fund that it was "a great and blessed . . . instrument . . . in its endeavour to establish a new home in the ancient land of our fathers".[21] Yerushalmi rehearses both Freud's comings and goings subtly as well, and he painstakingly shows that Freud's Jewishness runs the entire gamut from his identity as a Jew, arising from stubborn resistance to the "compact majority", through the whole process of recalling and accepting the tradition that develops out of Moses (and hence of reconciliation with the slain father), to the grandest idea of all: that in an act of sublimation peculiar to mono-theistic religion (borrowed from Egypt: Freud can't resist inserting that phrase), Jews subordinated sense perception to the spirit, disdained magic and mysticism, were invited "to advances in intellectuality" (I take this phrase from Strachey's translation, since it is inexplicably left out by Jones: the German word is *Geistigkeit*), and "were encouraged to progress in spirituality and sublimations". The rest of that progress, however, is yet to come in rather less evenly happy forms: "The people, happy in their conviction of possessing truth, overcome by consciousness of being the chosen, came to value highly all intellectual and ethical achievements. I shall also show how their sad fate, and the disappointments reality had in store for them, were able to strengthen all these tendencies."[22]

An even more detailed analysis of the relationship between Freud's Jewish identity and his quite convoluted attitudes, as well as actions, *vis-à-vis* Zionism is presented by Jacquy Chemouni in *Freud et le sionisme: terre psychanalytique, terre promise.*[23] Although Chemouni's conclusion is that Herzl and Freud divided the Jewish world between them – the former locating Jewishness in a specific location, the latter choosing instead the realm of the universal – the book presents a daring thesis about Rome, Athens and Jerusalem that comes quite close to Freud's antithetical views about the history and future of Jewish identity. Rome, of course, is the visible edifice that attracted Freud – perhaps, says Chemouni, because he saw in the city the destruction of Jerusalem's temple and a symbol of the Jewish people's exile and, as a result, the beginning of a desire to rebuild the temple in Palestine. Athens was a city of the mind, a generally more adequate representation of Freud's lifelong dedication to intellectual achievement. From that vantage point, the concrete Jerusalem is an attenuation of the spiritual ascetic ideal, even if it is also a realization that loss can be addressed through the concerted labour that was in fact Zionism.

What I find interesting – whether we accept Yerushalmi's sophisticated reclamation of Freud as a Jew forced to accede to his people's reality in Fascist Europe and anti-Semitic Vienna in particular, or Chemouni's somewhat more complex (a trifle fanciful?) and largely unresolved triangulation of the dilemma of exile and belonging – is that one element keeps importuning, and nagging at whoever thinks about these issues of identity in either uniformly positive or negative terms. And that element is the issue of the non-Jew, which Freud treats lackadaisically late in *Moses and Monotheism*. Jews, he says, have always attracted popular hatred, not all of which is based on reasons as good as the charge that they crucified Christ. Two of the reasons for anti-Semitism

are really variations on each other: that Jews are foreigners, and that they are "different" from their hosts; the third reason Freud gives is that no matter how oppressed Jews are, "they defy oppression, [so] that even the most cruel persecutions have not succeeded in exterminating them. On the contrary, they show a capacity for holding their own in practical life, and where they are admitted, they make valuable contributions to the surrounding civilization". As for the charge of Jews being foreigners (the implied context is, of course, European), Freud is dismissive of it, because in countries like Germany, where anti-Semitism is pervasive, the Jews have been there longer, having arrived with the Romans. On the accusation that Jews are different from their hosts, Freud backhandedly says that they are not "fundamentally so", since they are not "a foreign Asiatic race, but mostly consist of the remnants of Mediterranean peoples and inherit their culture".[24]

In the light of Freud's early harping on Moses's Egyptianness, the distinctions he makes here strike me as limp: both unsatisfactory and unconvincing. On several occasions Freud described himself, so far as language and culture were concerned, as German, and also Jewish; and throughout his correspondence and scientific writings he shows himself to be quite sensitive to issues of cultural, as well as racial and national difference. To the pre-Second-World-War European, though, the term "non-European" is a relatively unmarked term denoting people who come from outside Europe — Asiatics, for example. But I am convinced that Freud was aware that simply saying of the Jews that they were the remnants of Mediterranean civilization, and therefore not really different, is janglingly discordant with his show of force about Moses's Egyptian origins. Could it be, perhaps, that the shadow of anti-Semitism spreading so ominously over his world in the last decade of his life caused him protectively to huddle the Jews inside, so to speak, the sheltering realm of the European?

But if we move forward very rapidly from the immediate pre- to the post-World-War-Two period, we shall immediately take note of how designations like "European" and "non-European" dramatically acquire more sinister resonances than Freud appeared to have been aware of. There is, of course, the charge made by National Socialism, as codified in the Nuremberg Laws, that Jews were foreign, and therefore expendable. The Holocaust is a ghastly monument, if that is the right word, to that designation and to all the suffering that went with it. Then there is the almost too-perfect literalization that is given the binary opposition Jewversus-non-European in the climactic chapter of the unfolding narrative of Zionist settlement in Palestine. Suddenly the world of *Moses and Monotheism* has come alive in this tiny sliver of land in the Eastern Mediterranean. By 1948 the relevant non-Europeans were embodied in the indigenous Arabs of Palestine and, supporting them, Egyptians, Syrians, Lebanese and Jordanians who were descendants of the various Semitic tribes, including the Arab Midianites, whom the Israelites had first encountered south of Palestine and with whom they had a rich exchange.

In the years after 1948, when Israel was established as a Jewish state in Palestine, what had once been a diverse, multiracial population of many different peoples – European and non-European, as happened to be the case – there occurred anew a re-schematization of races and peoples, which, to those who had studied the phenomenon in nineteenth- and twentieth-century Europe, seemed like a parodistic re-enactment of the divisions that had been so murderous before. In this setting, Israel was internationally adopted by the Atlantic West (in fact had already been granted early title to Palestine by the Balfour Declaration of 1917) as, in effect, a quasi-European state whose fate, it seemed – in an eerie asseveration of the Fanonist argument, was to hold non-European indigenous peoples at bay for as long as possible.

The Arabs joined the non-aligned world, which was undergirded by the global struggle against colonialism as described by Fanon, Cabral, Nkrumah and Césaire. Inside Israel, the main classificatory stipulation was that it was a state for Jews, whereas non-Jews, absent or present as so many of them were, were juridically made foreigners, despite prior residence there. For the first time since the destruction of the Second Temple, the consolidation of Jewish identity occurred in the ancient place which, as it had been during biblical times, was occupied by several other nations, races, peoples, now made foreign or driven into exile, or both.

You see, perhaps, where I am going. For Freud, writing and thinking in the mid-1930s, the actuality of the non-European was its constitutive presence as a sort of fissure in the figure of Moses – founder of Judaism, but an unreconstructed non-Jewish Egyptian none the less. Jahveh derived from Arabia, which was also non-Jewish and non-European. Yet the Egyptian realities that were contemporary with Freud, as well as Egypt's plentiful antique history – exactly as for Verdi writing *Aïda* – were of interest because they had been mediated and presented for use by European scholarship, principally by way of Ernest Sellin's book on which *Moses and Monotheism* draws so abundantly.[25] There's an almost too perfect symmetry in the fact that Naguib Mahfouz, Egypt's great narrative genius, writes a novel about Akhenaten, *Dweller in Truth*,[26] which is as complex as any story he writes, but although there are many points of view explored in order to understand retrospectively who Akhenaten was, there is no mention at all of the incipient Jewish presence in the man Moses. The novel is as resolutely Egyptian as Israel was to be Jewish.

I very much doubt that Freud imagined that he would have non-European readers, or that in the context of the struggle over Palestine, he would have Palestinian readers. But he did and does. Let us look quickly at what becomes of his excavations – both figuratively and literally – from this new set of unexpectedly turbulent, as well as startlingly relevant, perspectives. I would say, first of all, that out of the travails of specifically European anti-Semitism, the establishment of Israel in a non-European territory consolidated Jewish identity politically in a state that took very specific legal and political positions effectively to seal off that identity from anything that was non-Jewish. By defining itself as a state of and for the Jewish people, Israel allowed exclusive immigration and land-owning rights there for Jews

only, even though there were former non-Jewish resi-
dents and present non-Jewish citizens whose rights were
attenuated in the case of the latter, abrogated retrospectively in the case of the former. Palestinians who
lived in pre-1948 Palestine can neither return (in the
case of the refugees) nor have access to land as Jews can.
Quite differently from the spirit of Freud's deliberately
provocative reminders that Judaism's founder was a non-
Jew, and that Judaism begins in the realm of Egyptian,
non-Jewish monotheism, Israeli legislation counter-
venes, represses, and even cancels Freud's carefully
maintained opening out of Jewish identity towards its
non-Jewish background. The complex layers of the past,
so to speak, have been eliminated by official Israel. So –
as I read him in the setting of Israel's ideologically
conscious policies – Freud, by contrast, had left considerable room to accommodate Judaism's non-Jewish
antecedents and contemporaries. That is to say: in
excavating the archaeology of Jewish identity, Freud
insisted that it did not begin with itself but, rather, with
other identities (Egyptian and Arabian) which his
demonstration in *Moses and Monotheism* goes a great
distance to discover, and thus restore to scrutiny. This
other non-Jewish, non-European history has now been
erased, no longer to be found in so far as an official

Jewish identity is concerned.

More relevant, I think, is the fact that by virtue of one of the usually ignored consequences of Israel's establishment, non-Jews – in this case, Palestinians – have been displaced to somewhere where, in the spirit of Freud's excavations, they can ask what became of the traces of their history that had been so deeply implicated in the actuality of Palestine before Israel? For an answer, I want to turn from the realm of politics and law to a domain much closer to Freud's account of how Jewish monotheism originated. I think I am right in surmising that Freud mobilized the non-European past in order to undermine any doctrinal attempt that might be made to put Jewish identity on a sound foundational basis, whether religious or secular. Not surprisingly, then, we will find that when Jewish identity has been consecrated by the establishment of Israel, it is the science of archaeology that is summoned to the task of consolidating that identity in secular time; the rabbis, as well as the scholars specializing in "biblical archaeology", are given sacred history as their domain.[27] Note that a huge number of commentators on and practitioners of archaeology – from William Albright and Edmund Wilson to Yigal Yadin, Moshe Dayan, and even Ariel Sharon – have noted that archaeology is *the* privileged Israeli science *par excellence*. As Magen Broshi, a noted Israeli archaeologist put it:

> The Israeli phenomenon, a nation returning to its old-new land, is without parallel. It is a nation in the process of renewing its acquaintance with its own land and here archeology plays an important role. In this process archeology is part of a larger system known as *yedi'at ha-Aretz*, knowledge of the land (the Hebrew term is derived most probably from the German *Landeskunde*). ... The European immigrants found a country to which they felt, paradoxically, both kinship and strangeness. Archeology in Israel, a *sui generis* state, served as a means to dispel the alienation of its new citizens.[28]

Thus archaeology becomes the royal road to Jewish-Israeli identity, one in which the claim is repeatedly made that in the present-day land of Israel the Bible is materially realized thanks to archaeology, history is given flesh and bones, the past is recovered and put in dynastic order. Such claims, of course, uncannily return us not just to the archival site of Jewish identity as explored by Freud, but to its officially (we should also not fail to add: its forcibly) sanctioned geographical

locale, modern Israel. What we discover is an extra-ordinary and revisionist attempt to substitute a new positive structure of Jewish history for Freud's *insistently* more complex and discontinuous late-style efforts to examine the same thing, albeit in an entirely diasporic spirit and with different, decentring results.

This is a good moment to say that I am greatly indebted to the work of a young scholar, Nadia Abu el-Haj, whose major book is entitled *Facts on the Ground: Archeological Practice and Territorial Self-Fashioning in Israeli Society*. What she provides first of all is a history of systematic colonial archaeological exploration in Palestine, dating back to British work in the mid-nineteenth century. She then continues the story in the period before Israel is established, connecting the actual practice of archaeology with a nascent national ideology – an ideology with plans for the repossession of the land through renaming and resettling, much of it given archaeological justification as a schematic extraction of Jewish identity despite the existence of Arab names and traces of other civilizations. This effort, she argues convincingly, epistemologically prepares the way for a fully fledged post-1948 sense of Israeli-Jewish identity based on assembling discrete archaeological particulars – scattered remnants of masonry, tablets, bones, tombs, etc. – into a sort of spatial biography out of which Israel emerges "visibly and linguistically, as the Jewish national home".[29]

More significantly, she argues that this quasi-narrative biography of a land enables – if it does not actually cause – and goes hand in hand with a particular style of colonial settlement that governs such concrete practices as the use of bulldozers, the unwillingness to explore non-Israelite (e.g. Hasmonean) histories, and the habit of turning an intermittent and dispersed Jewish presence of scattered ruins and buried fragments into a dynastic continuity, despite evidence to the contrary and despite evidence of endogamous non-Jewish histories. Wherever there is overwhelming and unavoidable evidence of a multiplicity of other histories, as in the massive palimpsest of Jerusalem's Byzantine, Crusader, Hasmonean, Israelite, and Muslim architecture, the rule is to frame and tolerate these as an aspect of Israeli liberal culture, but also to assert Israel's national pre-eminence by hitting at the Orthodox Jewish disapproval of modern Zionism by making Jerusalem even more of a Jewish-national site.[30]

Abu el-Haj's meticulous deconstruction of Israeli archaeology is also a history of the negation of Arab Palestine which, for obvious reasons, has been regarded as not worthy of similar investigation. But with the emergence of post-Zionist revisionist history in Israel during the 1980s and, simultaneously, the gradual rise of Palestinian archaeology as a practice in the liberation struggle of the past twenty or so years, the heritage-style attitudes of an exclusively biblical archaeology are now being challenged. I wish I had the time to go into this here, and to discuss how the nationalist thesis of separate Israeli and Palestinian histories has begun to shape archaeological disputes in the West Bank, and how, for instance, Palestinian attention to the enormously rich sedimentations of village history and oral traditions potentially changes the status of objects from dead monuments and artifacts destined for the museum, and approved historical theme parks, to remainders of an ongoing native life and living Palestinian practices of a sustainable human ecology.[31]

Nationalist agendas, however, tend to resemble each other, especially when different sides in a territorial contest look for legitimacy in such malleable activities as reconstructing the past and inventing tradition. Abu el-Haj is therefore quite right to suggest that despite the prevalence of an underlying Enlightenment commitment to the unity of the sciences, they are really quite disunited in practice. You can immediately grasp the ways in which archæology in the Israeli and the Palestinian context is not the same science. For an Israeli, archæology substantiates Jewish identity in Israel and rationalizes a particular kind of colonial settlement (i.e. a fact on the ground); for a Palestinian, archæology must be challenged so that those "facts" and the practices that gave them a kind of scientific pedigree are opened to the existence of other histories and a multiplicity of voices. Partition (as envisaged by the Oslo process since 1993) doesn't eliminate the contest between competing national narratives: rather, it tends to underline the incompatibility of one side with the other, thereby increasing a sense of loss and the length of the list of grievances.

Let me return finally to Freud and his interest in the non-European as it bears on his attempt to reconstruct the primitive history of Jewish identity. What I find so compelling about it is that Freud seems to have made a special effort never to discount or play down the fact that Moses was non-European – especially since, in the terms of his argument, modern Judaism and the Jews were mainly to be thought of as European, or at least belonging to Europe rather than Asia or Africa. We must once again ask: why? Certainly Freud had no thought of Europe as the malevolent colonizing power

described a few decades later by Fanon and the critics of
Eurocentrism, and except for his prophetic comment
about angering the Palestinian Arabs by giving undue
importance to Jewish monuments, he had no idea at all
of what would happen after 1948, when Palestinians
gradually came to see that the people who arrived from
abroad to take and settle on their land seemed just like
the French who came to Algeria: Europeans who had
superior title to the land over the non-European natives.
Neither – except very briefly – did Freud pause over how
strong and often violent the reaction of decidedly non-
European Arabs might have been to the forcible embodiment of Jewish identity in the nationalist fulfilment of
Judaism by the Zionist movement. He admired Herzl,
but I think it is correct to say that most of the time he
hesitated – indeed, he equivocated – so far as Zionism
itself was concerned. From an instrumental point of
view, Moses had to be a non-European so that in mur-
dering him the Israelites would have something to
repress, and also something to recall, elevate and spir-
itualize during the course of their great adventure in the
rebuilding of Israel overseas. That is one way to interpret
what Yerushalmi calls Freud's interminable Judaism:
that it was condemned to remember what it could not
easily forget, but that it pressed on with making Israel

stronger and more powerful none the less.

But that, I think, is not the only interpretative option. Another, more cosmopolitan one is provided by Isaac Deutscher's concept of the non-Jewish Jew. Deutscher argues that a major dissenting tradition within Judaism is constituted by heretical thinkers like Spinoza, Marx, Heine and Freud; these were prophets and rebels who were first persecuted and excommunicated by their own communities. Their ideas were powerful critiques of society; they were pessimists who believed that scientific laws governed human behaviour; their thinking was dialectical and conceived of reality as dynamic, not static, and human reality for them was (as in Freud's case) typified by the *homme moyen sensuel* "whose desires and cravings, scruples and inhibitions, anxieties and predicaments are essentially the same no matter to what race, religion, or nation he belongs"; they "agree on the relativity of moral standards", giving no one race, or culture, or God a monopoly of reason or virtue; finally, Deutscher says, they "believed in the ultimate solidarity of man", even though in the late twentieth century the horrors of our time compelled Jews to embrace the nation-state (which is "the paradoxical consummation of the Jewish tragedy"); even though, as Jews, they had once preached "the interna-

tional society of equals as the Jews were free from all
Jewish and non-Jewish orthodoxy and nationalism".[32]

Freud's uneasy relationship with the orthodoxy of his
own community is very much a part of the complex of
ideas so well described by Deutscher, who forgets to
mention what I think is an essential component of it: its
irremediably diasporic, unhoused character. This is a
subject which George Steiner has celebrated with great
élan for many years. But I would want to qualify
Deutscher by saying that this needn't be seen only as a
Jewish characteristic; in our age of vast population
transfers, of refugees, exiles, expatriates and immigrants,
it can also be identified in the diasporic, wandering,
unresolved, cosmopolitan consciousness of someone who
is both inside and outside his or her community. This is
now a relatively widespread phenomenon, even though
an understanding of what that condition means is far
from common. Freud's meditations and insistence on the
non-European from a Jewish point of view provide, I
think, an admirable sketch of what it entails, by way of
refusing to resolve identity into some of the nationalist
or religious herds in which so many people want so
desperately to run. More bold is Freud's profound
exemplification of the insight that even for the most
definable, the most identifiable, the most stubborn

communal identity – for him, this was the Jewish identity – there are inherent limits that prevent it from being fully incorporated into one, and only one, Identity.

Freud's symbol of those limits was that the founder of Jewish identity was himself a non-European Egyptian. In other words, identity cannot be thought or worked through itself alone; it cannot constitute or even imagine itself without that radical originary break or flaw which will not be repressed, because Moses was Egyptian, and therefore always outside the identity inside which so many have stood, and suffered – and later, perhaps, even triumphed. The strength of this thought is, I believe, that it can be articulated in and speak to other besieged identities as well – not through dispensing palliatives such as tolerance and compassion but, rather, by attending to it as a troubling, disabling, destabilizing secular wound – the essence of the cosmopolitan, from which there can be no recovery, no state of resolved or Stoic calm, and no utopian reconciliation even within itself. This is a necessary psychological experience, Freud says, but the problem is that he doesn't give any indication of how long it must be tolerated or whether, properly speaking, it has a real history – history being always that which comes after and, all too often, either overrides or represses the flaw. The questions Freud therefore leaves us with are: can so utterly indecisive and so deeply undetermined a history ever *be* written? In what language, and with what sort of vocabulary?

Can it aspire to the condition of a politics of diaspora life? Can it ever become the not-so-precarious foundation in the land of Jews and Palestinians of a bi-national state in which Israel and Palestine are parts, rather than antagonists of each other's history and underlying reality? I myself believe so – as much because Freud's unresolved sense of identity is so fruitful an example, as because the condition he takes such pains to elucidate is actually more general in the non-European world than he suspected.

INTRODUCING JACQUELINE ROSE

Christopher Bollas

There is something bizarre about travelling to a country where you do not belong, in the sense of having no lived connection, not for me, not in my family's past, a country to which I was not therefore returning, but where to say that much is already, in the eyes of the country itself, grounds for reproach. Not to return as a Jewish woman to Israel, not to feel a sense of belonging, not to recognise the very fact and existence of Israel as in itself a historic return, is to break on each count the symbolic parameters of the nation. ... This is a nation which desires its potential citizens exiled, diaspora Jewry, to come home, with as much fervour as it banishes the former occupants of its land from their own dream of statehood.

So writes Jacqueline Rose in her book *States of Fantasy*. Like Edward Said, Rose makes this observation to establish a transforming perspective, and it is from here that she critiques certain postmodernist perspectives: "I think it is for this reason that talk of the postmodern predicament belonging everywhere and nowhere at the same time has never felt quite right. There is something about this vision of free-wheeling identity which seems bereft of history and passion."[33]

Professor Rose's "Clarendon Lectures", delivered in 1994, are partly structured by her response to two events – the 1993 Israel–PLO peace treaty and the first non-racial elections in South Africa in 1994 – and she applies her own unique psychoanalytical perspective to discuss how fantasy conducts "itself" in the affairs of state; or – as she proposes, with characteristic lucidity: "psychoanalysis can help us to understand the symptom of statehood, why there is something inside the very process upholding the state as a reality which threatens and exceeds it".[34]

Rose often positions psychoanalysis in terms of feminine sexuality, and over the years she has established herself as one of the leading feminist critics of our time. Like Edward Said, she writes with a lyrical confrontation of those writers and issues which she opposes, but never from a sanctimonious posture – only ever as the writing of thought, of writing as engagement, not as riddance. Even when she deconstructs our pleasure in the story of Peter Pan, she gives something back, just as she takes something away: "Peter Pan is a front, a cover, not a concealer but as a vehicle for what is most unsettling and uncertain about the relationship between adult and child. It shows innocence not as a property of childhood but as a portion of adult desire."[35]

Rose is the author of six books: *Feminine Sexuality: Jacques Lacan and the école freudienne* (with Juliet Mitchell); *The Case of Peter Pan or the Impossibility of Children's Fiction*; *Sexuality in the Field of Vision*; *The Haunting of Sylvia Plath*; *Why War?*; *States of Fantasy*; *Jacques Lacan and the Question of Psychoanalytic Training* (which she translated); and most recently her widely acclaimed first novel, *Albertine*.[36]

Her students, colleagues and friends find in Jacqueline Rose a person of meticulous vision, who expresses difference as an act of great care as we shall see in her discussion of Professor Said's talk. For this and other aspects of her personal generosity, we thank her for her discussion this evening and her participation in this event.

Jacqueline Rose is Professor of English at Queen Mary and Westfield College, University of London.

RESPONSE TO EDWARD SAID

Jacqueline Rose

E dward Said's relation to Freud goes back a long way – probably, in fact, to long before the beginning in his writing which I associate with, appropriately enough, *Beginnings*, his magisterial study of literary genesis, which appeared in the States in 1975 but was first published in Britain a mere four years ago. In a long section devoted to *The Interpretation of Dreams*, he already analyses Freud's struggle with the genesis and writing of his own text. How can Freud authorize a "type of knowledge so devastating as to be unbearable in one's sight, and only slightly more bearable as a subject of psychological interpretation"?[37]

Returning to Freud today – and he will correct me if there have been other returns – Edward Said has offered us *Moses and Monotheism* as nothing less than a political parable for our times. In a gesture of stunning audacity – as I see it – and unquestionable brilliance, which will have surprised nobody here, Said has told us this evening that Freud's partial, fragmented, troubled, and at times self-denying relationship to his own Jewishness can provide a model for identity in the modern world. Freud did not live to see the full horrors of the Second World War. Nor, perhaps even more significantly in this context, did he witness the founding and subsequent history of the state of Israel, and the turmoil which its creation and existence have introduced into the land of Palestine. But with uncanny prescience, Freud – in his vision of a people brought into being by a stranger – offers an advance challenge to what is most intransigent in present-day Israel's relationship both to the Palestinians and to itself. To put it at its simplest: in Said's reading, as I understand it, *Israel represses Freud*. These lines come from near the end of the lecture:

> Quite differently from the spirit of Freud's deliberately provocative reminders that Judaism's founder was a non-Jew, and that Judaism begins in the realm of Egyptian, non-Jewish monotheism, Israeli legislation *countervenes*, *represses*, and *even cancels* Freud's carefully maintained opening out of Jewish identity towards its non-Jewish background. The complex layers of the past ... have been *eliminated* by official Israel.

By reading Freud in this way, Said has also offered us an exemplary performance of the model of reading which he defends early in the lecture (defends also, we might add, against some of his own critics). You read a historic writer not for what they failed to see, not for the ideological blindspots of their writing – too easy, too programmatic in the literary academy of recent years – but for the as-yet-unlived, still-shaping history which their vision – which must mean including the limitations of that vision – partially, tentatively, foresees and provokes. The task of such a reading is to "dramatize the latencies in a prior figure or form that suddenly illuminate the present". This is history, to use Walter Benjamin's famous expression, seizing "hold of a memory as it flashes up at a moment of danger". "For every image of the past", writes Benjamin, "that is not recognized by the present as one of its own concerns threatens to disappear irretrievably".[38] Said gives us a Freud in the present; or rather, "in a way that can only recall how Freud was and was not heard in his own time", he offers Freud to a present, to a world, or at the very least to "a tiny sliver of land in the Eastern Mediterranean", that will not listen.

A political parable, then, a model of reading, but no less powerfully, as I see it, a lament. Freud provides no consolation, no utopia – he was, of course, famous for this – but a fissure or wound at the heart of collective identity. In Said's words again, he "refuses to resolve identity into some of the nationalist or religious herds in which so many people want so desperately to run". In Said's hands, therefore, the "intransigent and irascible transgressiveness" of Freud's "late style" – which, perhaps not intentionally, sounds like a wonderful description of what many of us love most about Said himself – announces in the political domain what Freud declared so often to his patients: learn to live without consoling fictions, for in the death of such numbing and dangerous fantasies lies your only hope. We are talking here not about whole, nor even divided, but something more like *broken* identities. In a recent article, Marc Ellis, Professor of American and Jewish Studies at Baylor University, puts the question: "What if the centre of contemporary Jerusalem was seen as *broken* rather than salvific and *shared in that brokenness*, rather than divided by victory and defeat?"[39]

I find this vision inspiring, if difficult, and I share many of its ethical and political preoccupations. But, as a Jewish woman for whom Jewishness takes the form of an interminable questioning, I also have some questions – not exactly disagreements, which will perhaps be a source of disappointment for some of you and an immense relief for others, but questions which, I hope, might contribute to further debate. They turn first on Freud's relationship to his Jewishness, which Said characterizes as "hopelessly unresolved"; and secondly on this question of broken identities, and what Freud has to say in *Moses and Monotheism* about trauma – specifically about how trauma can lead not to the openness of diasporic identities, but to dogma and delusion instead.

Said puts it bluntly and, I believe, fairly when he remarks: "to say of Freud's relationship with Judaism that it was conflicted is to venture an understatement". For Said, the faultline in Freud's Jewish identity runs between his ability, in *Moses and Monotheism*, to conceive of Jewishness as grounded in a non-European – Egyptian – past and those other moments in his writing – which he describes as "limp: both unsatisfactory and unconvincing", "janglingly discordant" – when Freud seems, on the contrary, to be trying to establish the European credentials of the Jewish people as "not a foreign Asiatic race, but mostly [consisting] of the remnants of Mediterranean peoples and [inheriting] their culture". "I think I am right in surmising", Said puts it, "that Freud mobilized the non-European past in order to undermine any doctrinal attempt that might be made to put Jewish identity on a sound foundational basis." You could say, then, that Freud is never truer to himself than when he distances the Jew from his European affiliation. We could almost remove the "and" from the title of this lecture, "Freud *and* the Non-European", and read it instead as "Freud *the* Non-European". Or – to put it another way – through his complex, ambivalent relationship to his own Jewish identity, Freud, precisely as outsider, was able to tear away the façade of European perfectibility long before the horrors of the Second World War and the violence of anticolonial struggle would bring it crashing to the ground.

In the 1930 Hebrew preface to *Totem and Taboo*, Freud made this oft-cited statement:

No reader of [the Hebrew version of] this book will find it easy to put himself in the emotional position of an author who is ignorant of the language of holy writ, who is completely estranged from the religion of his fathers – as well as from every other religion – and who cannot take a share in nationalist ideals, but who has yet never repudiated his people, who feels that he is in his essential nature a Jew and who has no desire to alter that nature. If the question were put to him: "Since you have abandoned all these common characteristics of your countrymen, what is there left to you that is Jewish?" he would reply: "A great deal, and probably its very essence."[40]

Freud offers here one of the most striking self-definitions of the modern secular Jew — that is, the Jew for whom shedding the trappings of linguistic, religious and national identity — paradoxically, by stripping away its untenable and, one might say, most politically dangerous elements — does not make him less Jewish, but more. This is, as Deutscher — cited by Said — puts it, the non-Jewish Jew who lives in the interstices of the world. Except that this non-Jewish Jew — in this famous remark written in the same year that he refuses to support the founding of a Jewish state in Palestine — claims for himself the "essence" of Jewishness, sees himself in some sense as its custodian, fiercely lays claim to it as his possession, and believes, precisely through this claim to something he is incapable of putting into words, that the Jew has something specific to offer the world as a Jew. There was, as Dennis Klein points out in his *Jewish Origins of the Psychoanalytic Movement*,[41] a dilemma for the European and specifically Viennese Jew which can be traced back to the last years of the nineteenth century.

From the moment which can almost be dated to the day, 8 April, 1897, when the Emperor Franz Josef reluctantly confirmed the anti-Semite Karl Leuger as Mayor of Vienna, the emancipatory vision of the Viennese Jews ceased to be viable. In response to this loss, Viennese Jewry, according to Klein, adopted universalism as a specifically Jewish dream of freedom and justice which it was the task of Jews in general, and psychoanalysis in particular, to disseminate across the globe. You could almost say that, in this moment of historical failing which was among the first signs of the catastrophes to come half a century later, the Jew was the only true European left. Not only in response to the crisis of the 1930s, but much earlier (this was the period when he was delivering many of his papers in their preliminary draft form to B'Nai Brith), Freud believed – and some of the tensions described by Said can, I think, be traced to this belief – that it was the task of Jewish *particularity* to *universalize* itself.

In that contradictory impulse, we can also see one of the main lines of division inside the Zionism to which Freud would express his reluctant and belated allegiance in 1935. The division between what Arthur Hertzberg describes as "messianic" and "defensive" Zionism – the first believing that it was the destiny of Jews to enter into and complete the Enlightenment project by taking on the colours of the European nation-state, thereby demonstrating the "inevitable triumph of progress and liberalism" (Hertzberg calls it the "Jewish equivalent of the French revolution");[42] the second believing the opposite: that Zionism was the only viable option for Jews in the face of eternal anti-Semitism, a stain on the face of history which, giving the lie to any such dream of progress, endlessly repeats itself. Ahad Ha-Am was a Zionist who fervently opposed Herzl's political Zionism, and instead wanted Palestine to become the source of a spiritual renaissance for the Jew. In 1910, in words oddly similar to those of Freud's 1930 statement, he wrote: "Every true Jew, be he orthodox or liberal, feels in the depths of his being that there is something in the spirit of his people – *though we do not know what it is* – which has prevented us from following the rest of the world along the beaten path."[43]

I do not – let me stress in case you were beginning to wonder – share these beliefs, nor the Zionist vision for which both, in their competing ways, were to become the apology. But I do wonder whether Freud's relationship to his Jewishness, even more than Said has perhaps allowed, does not also partially bear their sign and their strain. In which case, it perhaps becomes harder to separate out the components of Freud's own Jewish identity, harder to pinpoint what is discordant and unconvincing. If – to quote Said again – Freud "mobilized the non-European past in order to undermine any doctrinal attempt that might be made to put Jewish identity on a sound foundational basis, whether religious or secular", there is equally a counter-current in his own thought which – although it cannot be retrieved in the same way for the urgencies of our political present – was none the less, for good, or rather bad, historical reasons – no less deeply and passionately felt.

What I am suggesting is that we move, in a sense, further along the path of Said's reading: that we should see Freud less as purely the diagnostician of – more squarely *inside* – the dilemma of identity which he describes. More simply, I am suggesting that the fixity of identity – for Freud, for any of us – is something from which it is very hard to escape – harder than Said, for wholly admirable motives, wants it to be. And on this subject, *Moses and Monotheism* also has a great deal to say. For if it offers an account, so brilliantly drawn out here this evening, of identities that know their own provisionality, it also does the opposite. In addition to bearing all the marks of late style so vividly characterized by Said – and, indeed, perhaps for that very reason – *Moses and Monotheism* is also one of Freud's most violent texts. *Moses and Monotheism* can, after all, be read as the story of a political assassination (in Freud's version, based on Sellin, the Jewish people kill their leader). It offers the thesis, already adumbrated in *Totem and Taboo*, that an act of murder is constitutive of the social tie. In fact monotheism, together with the "advance in intellectuality" that is said to accompany it, takes hold only because of the bloody deed which presided over its birth. As has often been pointed out, you can reject the flawed historical argument of both these texts while accepting the underlying thesis that there is no sociality without violence, that people are most powerfully and effectively united by what they agree to hate. What binds the people to each other and to their God is that they killed him.

It would be odd, then, if Freud himself was free of all the conflictual strains of identity to which, in this last work, he gives such potent and strange shape. What a people have in common, Freud suggests, is a trauma: "a knowledge" – to return to the quote from Said's *Beginnings* – "so devastating as to be unbearable in one's own sight, and only slightly more bearable as a subject of psychoanalytic investigation". This is, if you like, the other half of the story. For trauma, far from generating

freedom, openness to others as well as to the divided and
unresolved fragments of a self, leads to a very different
kind of fragmentation – one which is, in Freud's own
words, "devastating", and causes identities to batten
down, to go exactly the other way: towards dogma, the
dangers of coercive and coercing forms of faith. Are we at
risk of idealizing the flaws and fissures of identity?
Fragmentation can engender petrification, just as it can
be a consequence of historical alienation that a people,
far from dispersing themselves, start digging for a history to legitimate the violence of the state. "It is worth
specially stressing the fact", Freud writes on the return
of the repressed, "that each portion which returns from
oblivion asserts itself with peculiar force, exercises an
incomparably powerful influence on people in the mass,
and raises an irresistible claim to truth against which
logical objections remain powerless [. . .] This remarkable feature can only be understood on the pattern of the
delusions of psychotics."[44] Or – to put it more simply –
to be a social subject is to be, among other things, quite
mad.

In his discussion of archaeology, Edward Said con-
trasts Israeli archaeology, honed so as to consolidate the
Israeli citizens' belief in their fledgling state, and more
recent Palestinian archaeology's "attention to the enor-

mously rich sedimentations of village history", which challenges the first in the name of a "multiplicity of voices". As I listened to this moment of the lecture, I felt that one could almost say that Palestinian archaeology is the heir to Freud. I am less sanguine about the ability of new forms of nationalism to bypass the insanity of the group, especially given the traumatized history of both sides of the conflict in the Middle East. As Judge Richard Goldstone put it at the Ernest Jones Memorial Lecture in October, on the subject of the Albanians of Kosovo, we have an unrealistic expectation of how traumatized peoples will behave.

And I believe that Freud was less sanguine too – not only because, as Edward Said puts it, history represses the flaw, but because the most historically attested response to trauma is to repeat it. It is for similar reasons that I believe Freud to have been more torn between belonging and not belonging as a Jew, between his own remarkable vision of the Jew as created by a non-European and his belief in the Jew as the bravest – even the last – embodiment of the best of the spirit of Europe; between the Jew as eternal foreigner and the Jew as someone who wanted to enter the world of nations, who wanted – deluded or not – to go home. This evening, Edward Said has paid the most extraordinary tribute to

Freud by taking out of his last work a vision of identity as able to move beyond the dangers of identity in our times. If I dissent just a little, it is not just because I am not sure that Freud was quite there, but also because I wonder – as we look at the world around us today – whether any of us ever will be.

I want to end, however, on a different note. A year before Edward Said was due to give the 2001 Freud Memorial Lecture in Vienna – which was, as many of you will know, cancelled on the grounds of "the political conflict in the Middle East" – I was in Vienna speaking in the same annual event as part of a celebration of the centenary of *The Interpretation of Dreams*. The day after the event, which falls annually on Freud's birthday, Simon Rattle, in the first public commemoration of the Holocaust in Austria to date, was conducting the Viennese Philharmonic Orchestra at the site of the Mauthausen concentration camp. What was strangest about my visit was not only that coincidence but also the fact that my hosts seemed to want to talk, far more than about Freud and psychoanalysis, about the election of Haider and the resurgence of Austrian anti-Semitism (a traumatic resurgence, as one might say). To cancel Edward Said's lecture on political grounds in this con- text seems to me to be the saddest commentary on these anxieties and a missed opportunity, to say the least. I have stopped wishing that Edward Said could have been there, since the moment is so patently past or lost. But as I was reading his lecture and listening to him deliver it this evening, I certainly found myself wishing that some of those hosts could have been here.

NOTES

1. Edward W. Said, *Reflections on Exile and Other Essays*, Cambridge, MA: Harvard University Press 2001, p. 184.
2. Edward W. Said, *Joseph Conrad and the Fiction of Autobiography*, Cambridge, MA: Harvard University Press 1966.
3. Edward W. Said, *Orientalism*, New York, Pantheon Books 1978; *Beginnings: Intention and Method*, New York: Basic Books 1975, p. 39.
4. Edward W. Said, *The Question of Palestine*, New York: Times Books 1979.
5. Christopher Bollas, *Being a Character*, London: Routledge 1992, p. 207.
6. Said, *Reflections on Exile*, p. 186.
7. Edward W. Said, *Out of Place: A Memoir*, New York: Knopf 1999; *The End of the Peace Process: Oslo and After*, New York: Vintage 2000; *Power, Politics and Culture*, New York: Pantheon 2001.
8. Sigmund Freud, *Totem and Taboo*, trans. James Strachey, *Standard Edition*, Volume XIII, London: Hogarth Press 1955.
9. Sigmund Freud, *Moses and Monotheism*, trans. Katherine Jones, New York: Vintage 1967.
10. Frantz Fanon, *The Wretched of the Earth*, trans. Constance Farrington, New York: Grove Press 1968.
11. Ibid., p. 250.
12. Ibid., p. 301.

13. Ibid., pp. 311–12, 313.

14. Immanuel Wallerstein, "Eurocentrism and its Avatars: The Dilemmas of Social Science", *New Left Review* 226, November/December 1997, pp. 93–107.

15. See Richard H. Armstrong, "Freud: 'Schliemann of the Mind'", *Biblical Archeology Review*, March–April 2001.

16. See Janine Chasseguet-Smirgel, "Some Thoughts on Freud's Attitude During the Nazi Period", *Psychoanalysis and Contemporary Thought* 18:2 (1988), pp. 249–65.

17. Josef Hayim Yerushalmi, *Freud's Moses: Judaism Terminable and Interminable*, New Haven: Yale University Press 1991.

18. Ibid., pp. 52, 53; emphasis added.

19. Freud, *Moses and Monotheism*, p. 3.

20. Ibid., p. 39.

21. Yerushalmi, *Freud's Moses*, p. 13.

22. Quoted in ibid., pp. 108–9.

23. Jacquy Chemouni, *Freud et le sionisme: terre psychanalytique, terre promise*, Malakoff: Solin 1988.

24. Freud, *Moses and Monotheism*, p. 116.

25. Ernest Sellin, *Moses und Seine Bedeutung für die israelitische-jüdischer Religionsgeschichte*, Leipzig 1922.

26. Naguib Mahfouz, *Akhenaten: Dweller in Truth*, trans. T. Abu-Hassabo, New York: Anchor Books 1988.

27. See Keith W. Whitelam, *The Invention of Ancient Israel: The Silencing of Palestinian History*, London: Routledge 1996.

28. Quoted in Nadia Abu el-Haj, *Facts on the Ground: Archeological Practice and Territorial Self-Fashioning in Israeli Society*, Chicago: University of Chicago Press 2002, p. 48.

29. Ibid., p. 74.

30. See, in this context, Glenn Bowersock, "Palestine: Ancient History and Modern Politics", in Edward W. Said and Christopher Hitchens, eds, *Blaming the Victims: Spurious Scholarship and the Palestinian Question*, London and New York: Verso 1987. Strangely, this study is not mentioned by Abu el-Haj, who is otherwise

extremely thorough in her research.

31. See also the dramatic story told in Edward Fox, *Palestine Twilight: The Murder of Dr. Albert Glock and the Archeology of the Holy Land*, London: Harper Collins 2001.

32. Isaac Deutscher, *The Non-Jewish Jew and Other Essays*, New York: Hill and Wang 1968, pp. 35, 40.

33. Jacqueline Rose, *States of Fantasy,* Oxford: Clarendon Press 1996, p. 2.

34. Ibid., p. 10.

35. Jacqueline Rose, *The Case of Peter Pan or the Impossibility of Children's Fiction*, London: Macmillan 1984, p. xii.

36. Juliet Mitchell and Jacqueline Rose, *Jacques Lacan and the école freudienne*, London: Macmillan 1982; *The Case of Peter Pan or the Impossibility of Children's Fiction*; *Sexuality in the Field of Vision*, London: Verso 1986; *The Haunting of Sylvia Plath*, London: Virago 1991; *Why War? Psychoanalysis, politics and the return to Melanie Klein*, Oxford: Blackwell 1993; *States of Fantasy*, Oxford: Clarendon Press 1996; Moustapha Safouan, *Jacques Lacan and the Question of Psychoanalytic Training* translated and edited, London: Macmillan 2000; *Albertine*, London: Chatto 2001.

37. Said, *Beginnings*, p. 170.

38. Walter Benjamin, "These on the Philosophy of History", *Illuminations*, edited with an introduction by Hannah Arendt, translated by Harry Zohn, London: Fontana 1970, p. 257.

39. Marc Ellis, "The Boundaries of Our Destiny: A Jewish Reflection on the Biblical Jubilee on the Fiftieth Anniversary of Israel", in Naim Ateek and Michael Prior, eds, *Holy Land Hollow Jubilee – God, Justice and the Palestinians*, London: Melisende 1999, p. 244.

40. Freud, *Totem and Taboo: Some Points of Agreement between the Mental Life of Savages and Neurotics*, 1913, *The Standard Edition of the Complete Psychological Works of Sigmund Freud*, volume XIII, preface to the Hebrew edition, p. xv.

41. Dennis Klein, *Jewish Origins of the Psychoanalytic Movement*, London

and Chicago: University of Chicago Press 1985.

42. Arthur Hertzberg, *The Zionist Idea – A Historical Analysis and Reader*, Philadelphia and Jerusalem: Jewish Publication Society 1997, pp. 67, 63.

43. Ahad Ha-Am, cited in ibid., pp. 71–72 (emphasis mine).

44. Freud, *Moses and Monotheism: Three Essays*, 1939 [1934–38], *Standard Edition*, volume XXIII, p. 85.